One-Minute
Bible Stories
Old Testament

Other books by the author:
One-Minute Bedtime Stories
One-Minute Favorite Fairy Tales
One-Minute Animal Stories
One-Minute Bible Stories—New Testament
with Florence Henderson

One-Minute Bible Stories
Old Testament
Adapted by
Shari Lewis

Research by Gerry Matthews
Illustrated by C. S. Ewing

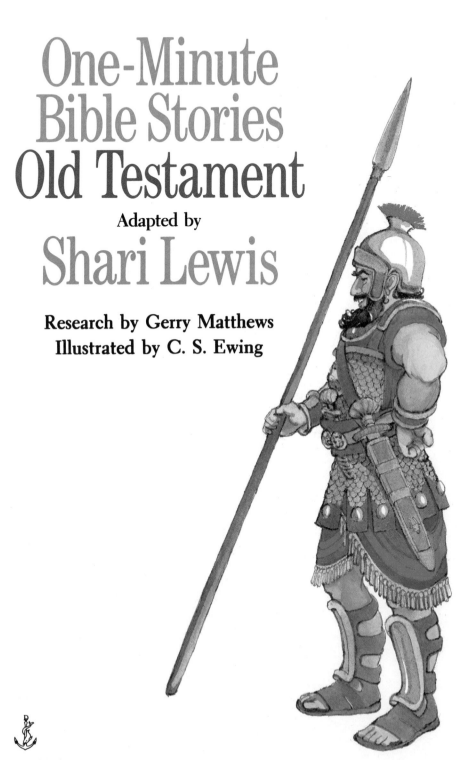

Doubleday
NEW YORK   LONDON   TORONTO   SYDNEY   AUCKLAND

To Saul Turtletaub and the tree that grew in the middle of Lake Ontario.

The author and the publisher gratefully acknowledge the assistance of the Reverend John F. Hartmann and Cantor Sanford D. Cohn in the preparation of this manuscript.

Published by Doubleday, a division of
Bantam Doubleday Dell Publishing Group, Inc.,
666 Fifth Avenue, New York, New York 10103.

Doubleday and the portrayal of an anchor with a dolphin
are trademarks of Doubleday, a division of
Bantam Doubleday Dell Publishing Group, Inc.

Library of Congress Cataloging-in-Publication Data

Lewis, Shari.
  One-minute Bible stories.

  Summary: Retells twenty well-known Old Testament
stories and parables in a simple, one-minute format,
from "Adam and Eve" to "Daniel in the Lions' Den."
  1. Bible stories, English—O.T. [1. Bible stories—O.T.]
I. Matthews, Gerry. II. Ewing, C. S., ill. III. Title.
BS551.2.L44 1986   221.9′505   86–2011
ISBN 0-385-19565-6 Trade
ISBN 0-385-19566-4 Prebound

4 6 8 9 7 5

Contents

Introduction

When I was a child, all the people in the Old Testament felt like family to me. Why not? I knew that my cousin Jud was just as flamboyant as the Judah Maccabee for whom he was named. Grandpa was as surely the patriarchal head of his group as Abraham *ever* was. And my sister and I were given the middle names of Ruth and Naomi, so we'd always be friends.

That's how I've approached these Old Testament tales. I've written in as concise a manner as I could, using lively, everyday language whenever possible, in order that the tales be really appealing and available for the young reader and listener.

However, in no way have I limited the word choice to short or particularly simple phrases. I find that kids grasp the meaning of new words quickly—without even asking—when those words are introduced naturally, in a context that fascinates them. I'm convinced that stories with a wide word choice help kids learn of the magical power of words to amuse, astound, to terrify or clarify. Once a child understands that these powers can belong to him or her, the youngster is likely to want the magic words and their controlling potentials for him or her self.

My editors and I had lots of discussions with Scripture scholars about which stories to include. We told "The Tower of Babel" and "Job"—rather tough tales of religious faith which are not normally introduced to the young child—because they *are* part of our literary heritage and pop up as conversational references. We felt that in this brief form at least the story line, if not the ultimate lesson, could be introduced and would be remembered, if not deeply comprehended.

The religious consultants urged that I not refer to the apple in "Adam and Eve," because the actual reference in the Scriptures is only to "the fruit of the tree of knowledge of good and evil." For the same reason, Joseph doesn't have a "coat of many colors," but rather "a long-sleeved coat," and Jonah is swallowed by "a very big fish," not a whale. So I've followed the advice of the experts consulted, and have stayed away from those specifics that were not originally in the Bible but have developed as part of popular legend.

In adapting these Bible stories, my hope is this: that the moral and story elements will become familiar to your youngsters, and the characters will feel like family—removed because of time, but recognized and beloved.

Shari Lewis

Adam and Eve

After five tiring days of creating the heavens and the earth, God gathered up some dust and molded a man, called him Adam, and put him in the Garden of Eden. Then God took a day off.

God told Adam he could eat anything in the Garden except the fruit on what was called the "Tree of Knowledge," because if he did, he would die. Adam said, "Fine!" and set about to name things. "That's a cow," said Adam. "And that's just got to be a pig."

Next, from Adam's rib God created a woman. Adam named her Eve, and together they played with the animals and ate sweet fruits from the trees.

One day the evil serpent hissed to Eve, "Why don't you ever eat any of—*those* fruits?", pointing to the juicy fruits on the Tree of Knowledge.

"I understand that's a no-no," she said. "They're dangerous."

"Nonsense!" said the serpent. So Eve talked Adam into sharing one of those fruits with her. Suddenly they realized they had done the *one* thing they weren't supposed to do.

Was God angry! He made Adam and Eve leave the Garden of Eden and go out into the world, where things weren't so easy. In fact, after a while Adam and Eve died. And God made the serpent crawl on his belly forever after.

Noah and the Ark

There were so many wicked people on earth, God decided to start again. He said to good, honest Noah, "It will rain until mountains disappear and there is nothing but water on earth. You must build an ark, a boat big enough to hold *your* family, plus two of every animal on earth."

So Noah built the ark and took aboard two of each creature, plus his wife, sons, and daughters-in-law.

It rained for forty days and nights until the ark floated alone on the watery surface of the earth.

Finally, God decided enough was enough and stopped the downpour. The ark came to rest on Mount Ararat, and Noah

sent out a dove. But finding only water, the dove flew back to the ark. Seven days later, Noah released the dove again. This time it returned with an olive branch in its beak, so Noah knew the water was going down and treetops were showing. And the next time the dove didn't return at all, which meant land was dry at last.

God said, "Obey my rules and I won't send another flood. To remind you, I'll put a rainbow in the sky when it rains."

Noah, his family, and all the animals went out to populate the earth once again . . . and boy, I'll bet it was muddy!

The Tower of Babel

Years after the great flood, all the people of the earth still spoke the same language and understood one another. They were proud when they realized that by working together, they could build a high tower. They decided to construct one so tall that it would reach up to God. They gathered wood and stones and made bricks out of clay and built a tower that reached into the heavens.

But when God saw the tower poking up into his heavens, He said, "They are so proud, they think they are as great as I am. If this is how they act, they will believe that nothing is beyond their power." So He studied the matter and decided what to do.

God figured that if they misunderstood one another, they couldn't possibly take orders or give them, so the tower would never be completed. God fixed it so the people suddenly spoke many *different* languages. Now, when friends and neighbors tried to talk to one another, there was nothing but confusion, for they didn't understand any language but their own. They stopped working on their tower and moved away to distant parts of the earth. There they built other cities, each with its own separate language. As years went by, these cities grew into countries, and the languages God had given them developed into the many languages spoken today.

13

Jacob's Ladder

Isaac and Rebekah had twin sons. Jacob was delicate, with smooth skin, while Esau's rough skin was covered with hair. Esau loved to hunt and fight. Jacob preferred to stay indoors and read. Jacob was his mother's favorite, but because Esau was born first he was supposed to inherit the land, the wealth, and his father's and God's blessings as well.

When time came for old Isaac to give the blessing, he was almost blind, so Rebekah dressed Jacob in his brother's coat and covered Jacob's smooth hands with goat hair. Jacob went to his father and said, "I am Esau." Isaac touched the coat Jacob was wearing, and knew that it was Esau's; he mistook the goat's hair on Jacob's hands for Esau's hairy hands. So Jacob received his father's blessing and everything else that should have gone

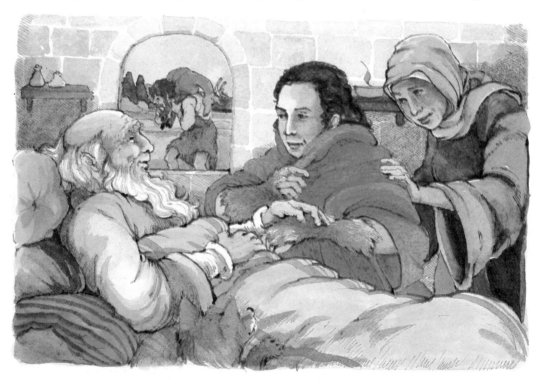

to his older brother.

When Esau found out, he was so mad that Rebekah sent Jacob off to live with his uncle in another land until Esau could calm down.

That night, sleeping with a rock for his pillow, Jacob dreamed that a bright ladder shone down to earth. On it, angels appeared and God, at the top, gave Jacob His blessing and said the land around him would be Jacob's and his children's forever. Jacob woke up, poured oil on his stone pillow, and named the place Beth-el, or God's House.

Joseph and His Wonderful Coat

Jacob had twelve sons, but he loved Joseph the most. When Joseph was seventeen, Jacob gave him an absolutely beautiful long-sleeved silk coat.

Joseph's older brothers were jealous of the wonderful coat *and* of all the attention Joseph got. They were even more upset when Joseph told them he had dreamed that someday his brothers would bow down before him and obey his commands.

One day Jacob sent his favorite son to the pasture to see how the sheep and goats were doing. The brothers were so angered at the sight of his beautiful coat that they took the coat away and threw Joseph into a deep pit without food or water.

They intended to kill him, but before they could, a camel caravan passed and the brothers sold Joseph into slavery. He was taken to Egypt.

To fool their father, the brothers splashed goat's blood on Joseph's coat. When Jacob saw it he thought Joseph had been killed by a wild beast, and he wept for days.

In Egypt the Ishmaelites sold Joseph to a captain of the Pharaoh's guard named Potiphar, and Joseph knew he would never see his home again.

Moses in the Bulrushes

A new Pharaoh came to rule Egypt who was afraid that the hardworking Hebrews would gain too much power and take over the kingdom.

He made the Hebrews his slaves and treated them like animals, sending them into the fields to dig ditches and carry heavy loads. But the Hebrews were a determined people, and their family life was strong.

Before long there were more of them than ever. "This isn't working," said Pharaoh. He ordered that every baby boy born to a Hebrew woman be killed.

Now one mother kept her newborn son hidden until he was three months old. Then she had the boy's sister, Miriam,

set the baby afloat in a little cradle amongst the bulrushes at the edge of the River Nile.

When Pharaoh's daughter came to bathe, she saw the tiny infant. "This must be one of the Hebrew babies," she said. "I'll hire a nursemaid to raise him." The child's sister, Miriam, was nearby, watching to make sure that her baby brother was safe. The Pharaoh's daughter asked Miriam to care for the baby. Pharaoh's daughter said, "I will call him Moses, and he will be raised in the palace as Pharaoh's grandson."

And so he was.

Moses and
the Burning Bush

As Moses grew up, he saw his people being treated badly. One day, trying to stop an Egyptian guard from beating a Hebrew worker in the fields, Moses killed the Egyptian.

Pharaoh sent his soldiers to kill Moses, who ran away to a land called Midian. There a kind priest offered him food and a place to sleep. Moses stayed and married the priest's

daughter Zipporah, and they had a son.

One day, tending sheep on Mount Horeb, Moses saw fire coming from a bush, but the bush wasn't burnt. Amazed, Moses said, "How can this happen?"

It was God in the burning bush, and He said, "Moses, go back to Egypt and tell Pharaoh to free the Hebrews so they can return to Israel, the land of milk and honey."

Moses was frightened. "Why would Pharaoh do what

I say?" he asked. "I'm nobody."

"Watch this," said God, and He turned the stick Moses was carrying into a wriggling snake. "Pick it up," said God. Moses grabbed the snake, and suddenly it was a stick again. God said, "If you'll do that, and other wonders I'll show you, Pharaoh *will* pay attention." So Moses set out for Egypt to save the Hebrews from slavery.

The Parting of the Red Sea*

Moses went back to Egypt to lead the Hebrews out of slavery. To impress Pharaoh, he performed marvels with the stick God had blessed. But Pharaoh wanted his slaves and absolutely, positively refused to let the Hebrews leave the country.

Moses waved the stick over the River Nile. The river turned to blood, and the Egyptians had no water to drink, but Pharaoh wouldn't give in.

Then God covered the land with lice, but Pharaoh still wouldn't budge.

With God's help, Moses caused one awful thing after another to happen. Finally, God killed all Egyptian firstborn children. That did it! Pharaoh gave up.

Moses was leading the Hebrews toward Israel when Pharaoh changed his mind. "What am I doing?" he said. "We need Hebrews to do the hard work around here!"

So Pharaoh sent his army to bring them back. But on the shores of the Red Sea,* Moses waved his stick. The waters parted, leaving a path, and the Hebrews walked across.

The soldiers followed, but the waves fell back and Pharaoh's whole army drowned. Moses and the Hebrews were free at last.

*Actually, though best known as the Red Sea, this was the Sea of Reeds.

Moses and the Ten Commandments

Moses climbed to the top of a mountain called Sinai to have a word with God, who reminded Moses that He'd brought the Israelites out of Egypt and looked after them. "I like you people," said God. "If you'll follow my rules, I'll see that no harm comes to you."

Then God spoke like thunder. "Here are two stone tablets with my Ten Commandments carved on them," said God. "Number One, you have to remember that I'm the only real God there is. Two, don't make any statues or pictures of false gods and bow down to them or I'll be angry. Three, do not take my name in vain. Four, the seventh day of the week is for resting, so don't work on that day. Take it easy, think about things. Five, always pay attention to your mother and father. Six, Seven, and Eight, never kill anybody, don't commit adultery, and please stop taking things that aren't yours. Nine, be

fair and truthful with friends and neighbors. Ten, don't be jealous of what other people have . . . be happy with what you've got."

Moses took the stone tablets down from the mountain and explained to the people what was written on them, and the Israelites promised to obey God's Ten Commandments forever.

The Ark of the Covenant

Moses brought the Israelites the stone tablets with the Ten Commandments carved on them, and they built a golden box in which to keep them, fitted with handles so it could be carried.

They called the box the ark of the covenant because it held the "covenant" or agreement God had made with them. Of course the ark was a holy object and the people kept it with them wherever they went.

But many years later, when the Israelites had almost forgotten about God, the ark was captured by the Philistines, taken to a temple in a Philistine city, and placed next to a stone statue of their god, Dagon. Next morning, the Philistines found

the statue with its head and hands broken off. Soon the Philistines became sick. Many died, so they sent the ark of the covenant to another city. There the same thing happened. The Philistines decided they had to get rid of it.

They placed the ark on a cart pulled by cows, and said, "If the cows take the cart to Israel, we will know it was God's power that made us suffer." The cows walked straight down the road to Israel, and when the Israelites saw the ark they swore never to forget about God again, and happiness came back to Israel.

Joshua and the Walls of Jericho

After Moses died, his assistant, Joshua, became the leader of the Hebrews. Following God's orders, Joshua told his people that all the land in Israel was theirs, and they must take possession of it.

First they came to the city of Jericho, surrounded by a stone wall. There, God spoke to Joshua. He said: "I am here to help you. Tell your soldiers to march around the city once each day for six days while seven priests blow their ram's horn trumpets. On the seventh day, have them march around *seven* times and at the end, let the priests blow one long blast. At the sound of this final trumpet note, the people must shout as loudly as they can, and the city will be yours."

Joshua told his army to do this, and when they heard the trumpets, they shouted so loudly that it sounded like God's own thunder, and the walls of the city of Jericho came tumbling down. Joshua led the Hebrews into the city, and it was theirs!

Gideon

The Israelites angered God by worshipping a stone idol called Baal, so God sent armies of Midianites to steal the people's grain and animals, and there was hardship in Israel.

One day, an angel of God told Gideon, "You must drive the Midianites out of Israel."

"Why can't God do that?" moaned Gideon. "He led the Israelites out of Egypt, why can't he help us now? I am a small man. How can *I* drive away a whole army?"

The angel said, "Tear down the statue of Baal, and in its place build an altar to God."

As soon as he did, Gideon felt the strength of God inside

him. To the Midianites' camp, he gathered a great army of the men of Israel.

God said, "You don't need all these people to defeat the Midianites."

So Gideon gave three hundred men each a trumpet, a jar, and a torch.

Surrounding the thousands of Midianites, the Israelites blew their trumpets and smashed their jars on the ground. The Midianites heard this awful racket and saw the three hundred torches burning around them. Thinking it must be a huge army to make so much noise, they ran away.

And Gideon let the people know that they had been saved not by Baal, but by God.

Samson and Delilah

At one time the Philistines ruled Israel, and they made slaves of everyone except Samson. Samson was so strong, he once killed a thousand soldiers with nothing but the jawbone of an ass, and the Philistines wanted to capture him.

They asked Delilah, Samson's girlfriend, to help them. "We will make you rich," they said. "Well," said she, "I'm fond of the big guy, but I could use some new clothes."

The next time Samson came to visit, Delilah asked him, "What would make you lose your strength? What is your secret?" Samson admitted, "If you shave my head, I'll be as weak as any man." She did, and it worked. The soldiers captured Samson and put out his eyes and made him a slave.

After a while, the Philistines decided to have a celebration.

They chained poor, blind Samson to the stone pillars of the temple so they could make fun of him. They poked at him and laughed and said, "You don't look like much now, Hebrew!" Nobody noticed that Samson's hair had grown back and along with it, his strength. When the temple was filled with laughing, jeering people, Samson pushed the pillars over. The roof of the temple fell in, and that was the end of the laughter—and, unfortunately, of Samson as well.

David and Goliath

Israel was again attacked by Philistines, so a shepherd named David left his father's flock and went to King Saul's camp to see if he could help.

Goliath, a giant Philistine warrior, stood alone on the battlefield, covered in armor and carrying a spear with an iron point bigger than David's head.

"Let any Israelite come out and fight!" bellowed the giant. "If you can kill me, the war will end and my soldiers will go home." The Israelites were afraid, but David said to King Saul, "*I* will kill the giant."

The king laughed. "Goliath can blow a boy like you away with a breath."

"I've killed lions with my slingshot when they attacked my father's sheep," David said. "If I can kill a lion, I can kill this overgrown Philistine."

34

The king saw that David had the spirit of God, so he agreed.

Carrying only his slingshot and a few stones, David walked onto the battlefield. The giant ran forward with his weapons raised. David quickly put a stone in his sling and pulled back as hard as he could. The little stone flew through the air like a bolt of lightning, struck Goliath in the forehead, and the giant fell dead at David's feet.

David and King Saul

David killed the giant Goliath, and of course he became famous. Wherever he appeared, people talked of his bravery. King Saul was jealous that the young giant killer was now a great hero. Saul was afraid of him, too, for he felt that David had the strength of God behind him.

The king sent the shepherd into many battles, hoping he'd be killed, but each time David was victorious and returned a bigger hero than ever.

Saul plotted to have David murdered, but David escaped into the wilderness, bewildered by his king's hatred.

King Saul searched the wilderness with three thousand soldiers, but they couldn't find David. That night they set up

camp and went to sleep.

From a distant hill, David saw the king's camp. He sneaked down and found Saul asleep, his spear beside him. "It would be easy to kill this sleeping man," David thought. "Then I would be safe again." But instead he sliced off a bit of the king's cloak, and took it and the king's spear back to his hilltop.

He called to the king and waved the spear. When King Saul saw his weapon, he knew David had spared his life, and he was touched. He vowed never to do him harm.

Later, after King Saul died, David became the second king of Israel.

The Wisdom of King Solomon

King David died, and his son Solomon became king of Israel. God asked the new king, Solomon, what he needed. Solomon pleased God because he didn't ask for riches, but rather for the wisdom to know right from wrong. God granted Solomon's wish.

The news of King Solomon's great wisdom spread, and people asked his advice.

One day two women arrived. "We live in the same house," said the first woman. "We each gave birth to a little boy, but one baby died." The second woman, who had an infant in her arms, said, "This one is mine." "No!" wailed the

first, "I know my son. He is mine!" and she wept.

Obviously both women could not be the mother of the same baby, so King Solomon picked up his sword and said, "There is a very simple solution to this problem. I'll cut this baby in half, and give half a baby to each of you."

"Sounds fair to me," said the second woman, happy at least that the *other* lady had not won. But the first woman cried, "Oh no, give the baby to *her*, my lord. I would rather lose my son than have him harmed."

Hearing this, Solomon gave the child to the first woman, for he could see that she loved the infant and was his true mother.

Jonah and the Huge Fish

In Nineveh, God was forgotten and people were mean to each other. Angered, God told Jonah to go to Nineveh and save the people from their wicked ways. Jonah was scared and didn't want to go, so he hopped on a ship sailing to Tarshish. "God won't find me in Tarshish," he said. "Nobody who is *anybody* goes there."

But God saw Jonah, and made a mighty storm at sea. The ship was in danger of sinking. The frightened sailors prayed to every idol they could think of, but the storm only got worse.

Jonah knew what God was doing. "If you'll throw me overboard," he said to the terrified sailors, "the winds will die down and the sea will be calm again." So they dumped Jonah

over the side, and in a flash the storm ended.

Now Jonah couldn't swim, and thought he was finished, but suddenly he was swallowed by a gigantic fish.

Jonah began to pray. Right from the belly of that fish, Jonah prayed for three days and nights. He promised to obey God's every command if only He'd let him live. On the fourth day God spoke, and the fish threw Jonah up onto a beach.

This time, when God told Jonah to go save the people of Nineveh, he went—quickly!

Job

Job was happy. He had a loving wife and ten children, and he lived on a big farm with thousands of sheep, camels, oxen, and everything else a man could want. God loved and admired Job so much, he often passed that way just to see how he was getting along.

One day, God saw Satan strolling nearby. "What about this man, Job?" asked God. "He is as good and honest as anyone on earth." Satan laughed. "Come on, God. That's easy for a man who's got everything. I'll bet if his life were harder he wouldn't be so nice." "It's a bet!" said God. "I'll allow you to make life hard for Job, and you'll see what he does."

So Satan caused Job to lose his animals. His servants were taken away. Poor Job was ruined, but didn't become angry with

God. He said, "I was born without anything and that's the way I'll die. The Lord gives, and the Lord takes it back; blessed be the Lord."

Next time God saw Satan, He said, "What did I tell you? Job is just as good and honest as he ever was." But Satan said, "I'll make him really sick and then we'll see." So Satan made Job so sick he wanted to die, but Job never stopped being good and honest.

God was truly pleased. He made Job well again and gave him twice as many animals and servants as before, and Job lived to be a hundred and forty, the happiest man in the land.

The Handwriting on the Wall

When King Nebuchadnezzar died, his son Belshazzar became king. But instead of minding his kingly business, Belshazzar gave big parties. And instead of worshipping God, he bowed down to false gods carved out of gold and silver.

One night, during one of Belshazzar's parties, a man's hand appeared. It was *just* a hand, without the rest of the body of the man, and it wrote mysterious words on the palace wall. *Mene, Mene, Tekel, Upharsin,* wrote the hand, and then it was gone.

Belshazzar was so frightened his knees knocked together. "What does it mean?" he demanded, but nobody had any idea. "Ask Daniel," someone suggested, for Daniel was known to be very wise.

Daniel said, "The word *Mene* means that the days of your kingdom are *numbered,* and will soon end. *Tekel* means that what you have done has been *weighed* on the scale and you have been found wanting. And *Upharsin* means that your land will be *divided* and given away."

And that very night, just as Daniel had predicted, Belshazzar was murdered, his land was divided and given away, and Daniel's fame as a wise man spread far and wide.

Daniel in the Lions' Den

King Darius so admired Daniel, he gave him power over the whole kingdom. This made the king's deputies jealous, and as they looked for a way to get rid of Daniel they remembered that God was even more important to Daniel than the king was. They said to Darius, "Great King, because we love you we think there should be a law that anyone caught praying to a ruler other than *you*, be it god or man, should be thrown to the lions." Flattered, Darius agreed.

Now the deputies watched until they caught Daniel praying to God, and they tattled to the king.

"I'm sorry, but a law is a law," the king told Daniel. "However, I *do* hope your God can save you, because I need you around here."

That night the deputies threw Daniel into a den with wild lions. Next morning Darius ordered the door of the den pushed away. There was Daniel, with a huge lion on top of him—*licking his face!* Daniel said, "An angel of God kept the lions from eating me. But if I don't get out soon, I'll be loved to death. This big cat's rough tongue is rubbing my skin off."

Happy King Darius took Daniel from the lions' den and instead threw in the deputies who had accused Daniel.

That day the lions loved the deputies, too—for lunch!